# Ripley Readers

*Learning to read. Reading to learn!*

## LEVEL ONE   **Sounding It Out**  Preschool–Kindergarten
For kids who know their alphabet and are starting to sound out words.

learning sight words • beginning reading • sounding out words

## LEVEL TWO   **Reading with Help**  Preschool–Grade 1
For kids who know sight words and are learning to sound out new words.

expanding vocabulary • building confidence • sounding out bigger words

## LEVEL THREE   **Independent Reading**  Grades 1–3
For kids who are beginning to read on their own.

introducing paragraphs • challenging vocabulary • reading for comprehension

## LEVEL FOUR   **Chapters**  Grades 2–4
For confident readers who enjoy a mixture of images and story.

reading for learning • more complex content • feeding curiosity

***Ripley Readers***  Designed to help kids build their reading skills and confidence at any level, this program offers a variety of fun, entertaining, and unbelievable topics to interest even the most reluctant readers. With stories and information that will spark their curiosity, each book will motivate them to start and keep reading.

**Vice President, Licensing & Publishing**  Amanda Joiner
**Editorial Manager**  Carrie Bolin

**Editor**  Jordie R. Orlando
**Designer**  Luis Fuentes
**Text**  Carrie Bolin
**Reprographics**  Bob Prohaska

**President**  Andy Edwards
**Chief Commercial Officer**  Brett Clarke
**Vice President, Global Licensing &**
  **Consumer Products**  Cassie Dombrowski
**Vice President, Creative**  Dov Ribnick
**Senior Athlete Manager**  Ricky Melnik
**Global Accounts & Activation Manager,**
  **Consumer Products**  Andrew Hogan
**Art Director & Graphic Designer**  Josh Geduld
**Special Thanks**  Bruce Cook

Published by Ripley Publishing 2019

10 9 8 7 6 5 4 3 2 1

Copyright © 2019 Nitro Circus

ISBN: 978-1-60991-281-9

No part of this publication may be reproduced in whole or in part, stored in a retrieval system, or transmitted in any form by any means, electronic, mechanical, photocopying, recording, or otherwise, without written permission from the publisher.

For more information regarding permission, contact:
VP Licensing & Publishing
Ripley Entertainment Inc.
7576 Kingspointe Parkway, Suite 188
Orlando, Florida 32819
Email: publishing@ripleys.com
www.ripleys.com/books

Manufactured in China in May 2019.

First Printing

Library of Congress Control Number: 2019903093

PUBLISHER'S NOTE
While every effort has been made to verify the accuracy of the entries in this book, the Publisher cannot be held responsible for any errors contained in the work. They would be glad to receive any information from readers.

WARNING
Some of the stunts and activities are undertaken by experts and should not be attempted by anyone without adequate training and supervision.

**PHOTO CREDITS**

**Cover** (bkg) © EFKS/Shutterstock.com; **5** © Mark Watson/nitrocircus.com; **22-23** (dp) © Chris Tedesco/Nitro Circus; **23** © Jon Currier Photography; **24** © Mark Watson/nitrocircus.com; **26-27** (dp) Tyler Tate/T Squared Action Sports; **28-29** (dp) © Mark Watson/nitrocircus.com; **30** © Chris Tedesco/Nitro Circus; **31** © Chris Tedesco/Nitro Circus

Key: t = top, b = bottom, c = center, l = left, r = right, sp = single page, dp = double page, bkg = background

All other photos are courtesy of Nitro Circus and Bruce Cook. Every attempt has been made to acknowledge correctly and contact copyright holders, and we apologize in advance for any unintentional errors or omissions, which will be corrected in future editions.

LEXILE®, LEXILE FRAMEWORK® , LEXILE ANALYZER®, the LEXILE® logo and POWERV® are trademarks of MetaMetrics, Inc., and are registered in the United States and abroad. The trademarks and names of other companies and products mentioned herein are the property of their respective owners. Copyright © 2019 MetaMetrics, Inc. All rights reserved.

# NITRO CIRCUS

## NEVER SAY CAN'T

FEATURING:
### *BRUCE COOK*

Bruce Cook loves riding motorcycles! He rides his motorcycle in shows with Nitro Circus.

Bruce's motto is "Never Say Can't!"

Bruce does not like the word "can't." He says, "If you want something bad enough, you'll figure it out."

A family farm in Kelowna, Canada, is where Bruce grew up. His dad and his grandpa often told him to never say "can't." That is something he never forgot.

Riding is something Bruce has always loved to do. He began riding dirt bikes when he was only five!

Bruce learned to ride FMX motorcycles at his family farm, too. He and his friend set up ramps. They practiced at the farm.

Then they started riding together in action sports shows.

Doing stunts on his motorcycle was Bruce's favorite thing to do! Soon, he started performing with his friends at Nitro Circus.

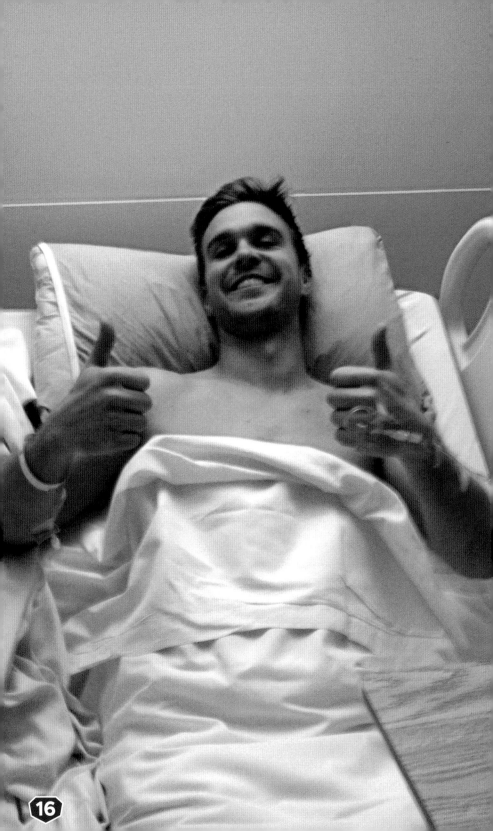

Bruce tried a stunt that no one had done before. He wanted to do the world's first double frontflip on a motorcycle.

But there was an accident. Bruce could no longer use his legs.

His friends and family were sad.
But Bruce was glad to be alive.
He knew he wanted to ride his
bike again. He never said can't!

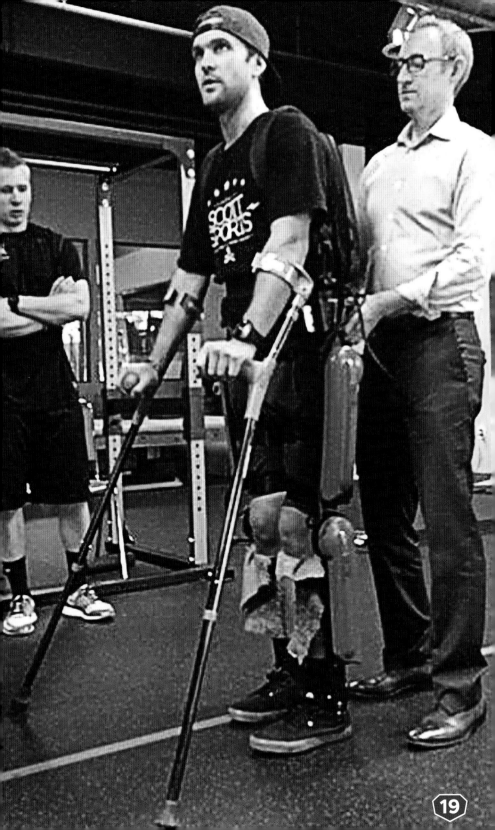

Bruce set a goal. He wanted to ride his motorcycle again before a year had passed.

It only took him nine months to reach his goal!

Now Bruce needed a special motorcycle to ride. Straps hold his feet and legs in place. A seat belt keeps him in his seat. Special bars keep him safe if he crashes.

The motorcycle worked! Bruce could ride again!

He set another goal. He wanted to be the first paraplegic person to do a backflip on a motorcycle.

He did it! Bruce reached his goal. The trick was successful. His friends and family cheered!

Bruce didn't listen when people told him he couldn't ride anymore. He found a way. He set goals. He didn't give up.

"There are always people telling you why you can't," says Bruce. "But it's up to you to stick to your goals."

# Never say can't!